P9-CUK-255

Baby showers

Baby showers

original ideas for an unforgettable day

AMY ELLIOTT

RYLAND
PETERS
& SMALL

LONDON NEW YORK

Senior Designer Toni Kay
Senior Editor Catherine Osborne
Picture Research Emily Westlake
Production Gemma John
Art Director Leslie Harrington
Publishing Director Alison Starling

First published in the United Kingdom
in 2008 by Ryland Peters & Small.
20–21 Jockey's Fields
London WC1R 4BW

519 Broadway, 5th Floor
New York, NY 10012
www.rylandpeters.com

10 9 8 7 6 5 4 3 2 1

ISBN: 978-1-84597-752-8

A catalogue record for this book is
available from the British Library.

Printed in China

Contents

Introduction

The birth of a child is a universally joyous occasion, and in most social circles, expecting mothers, and often both parents, are honored with a baby shower. Crocheted booties and frilly layettes aside, the modern shower has become more practical; most gifts are intended to help ease the financial strain that comes with furnishing a nursery and purchasing essentials like car seats and strollers. Delicious food and drink are still part of the deal (and yes, even the occasional game or activity).

As hostess of a baby shower, your mission is to organize this candy-colored show of moral support. The celebration should be tailored to the tastes of the expecting parents, but must also work for you, your budget, and the amount of time and creative energy you can devote to the task. This book contains the basic guidelines you'll need to get started, but feel free to improvise and put your own unique spin on this tradition.

Putting it together

Perfect timing

Plan to schedule the baby shower for some time during the last trimester of the mother-to-be's pregnancy; most hostesses select a Saturday or Sunday afternoon that's six to eight weeks before the baby's due date. Present a few dates to the mother-to-be and let her decide. To ensure the attendance of important friends and family, the mother-to-be should inform these people of the potential dates as soon possible (it's also appropriate for the shower hostess to conduct this "recon" herself) and take their availability into account when committing to a date. Once a day has been selected, it's courteous—though certainly not mandatory—to send out save-the-date cards or emails, especially if certain guests will be flying in from out of town. Save-the-dates will also be much appreciated if the shower is planned for a holiday weekend or during the summer vacation months.

The setting

Host the event in a venue that's conveniently located, at least for the showeree and the majority of guests. Traditionally, baby showers are held in a close friend or relative's home, though restaurants, tea houses and hotel function rooms are also

popular. Public beaches and parks are yet another option, although outdoor celebrations do require a little extra forethought and preparation, due to unpredictable weather and possible alcohol and noise regulations. You might also consider hosting the event at the home of the mother-to-be, thereby eliminating any need for her to travel. And she wouldn't have to transport a car-load of gifts to her home after the shower.

Also think about...

Formality Choose a venue that will accommodate the showeree's sense of formality—not necessarily your own. An elegant tea party in a chandelier-lit hotel lobby might strike you as a divine setting for the baby shower, but ignore these instincts if the showeree is a casual, backyard barbecue kind of girl. By the same token, a picnic on the beach would not suit a multi-generational, Chanel-wearing crowd.

Size The number of guests you're planning to have should guide you in your selection of the proper space. A small gathering will find it difficult to mingle in a sprawling hotel dining room—an intimate lounge with plush seating would feel infinitely more warm and inviting. Meanwhile, the showeree's cousin may be adamant about having the shower in her tiny apartment, but you'll have to convince her that such petite quarters cannot accommodate 100 guests.

Food If the venue is providing food and beverages for the shower, make sure you have sampled their offerings at some point or other, or at least have a recommendation from someone who can vouch for the quality. If you have any doubts, ask to schedule a tasting with the chef.

Invitations and guests

Who's invited to a baby shower? You're certainly not limited to a female-only crowd. Co-ed showers are quite commonplace and offer their own breed of fun and excitement. Not that the traditional women-only, desserts-and-punch variety is a total bore, but a gathering that consists of both male and female attendees will have the energy of a "regular" party—much less cute and cuddly, much more chic and contemporary.

Obtain a list of names and addresses from the expectant parents, and plan to have the invitations in the mail at least six weeks before the event.

The information you must include

Shower date

Names of the parents Even if it's a women-only shower, Dad usually makes an appearance at the very end to say "hello" (and help cart home gifts).

Time and duration Three to four hours is a sensible length for a baby shower.

Address Include a map/direction card insert; if the shower is to be held at a venue other than a private home, include its phone number and website.

The sex of the child Only if applicable—many parents want the sex to be a surprise.

Registry info The word-of-mouth route has served shower guests well enough for decades, but it's generally considered okay to include an insert that lists the stores and/or websites where the mother or parents have created registries. For example: *Gladys is registered at babygap.com and babiesRus.com.*

Hostess duties and responsibilities

In agreeing to host the baby shower, you're also expected to pay for the affair. While the cost of a bridal shower is split among bridesmaids, there's no default "posse" in place to help you shoulder the expenses of a baby shower. However, key people, like the showeree's parents, siblings and in-laws are likely to make contributions. Even if no one takes out his/her checkbook, you'll find that many guests will be happy to help you with the following:

- ❀ *Addressing and mailing the invitations*
- ❀ *Assembling the party favors*
- ❀ *Hanging decorations or arranging flowers*
- ❀ *Returning rentals*
- ❀ *Food pickup and/or preparation*
- ❀ *Gift organization*
- ❀ *Purchasing a guest book and making sure that everyone signs it*
- ❀ *Cleaning up before and after*
- ❀ *Taking photos*

At the actual event it will be up to you to manage the flow of the day, allowing sufficient time for games and activities and the opening of the gifts. The mother-to-be's comfort is also your responsibility, so make sure you have a nice, comfy chair for her to sit in (bring a pillow, if necessary) and make sure she drinks plenty of water.

Style & themes

Decorations

Baby shower décor often embraces the nature of the party in a literal way, from folding cloth napkins into diaper shapes to creating table centerpieces with baby bottles as vases. But you can certainly dress up the room as you would for any other party. Guests already know they're at a baby shower, so you have only to immerse them in an environment that's simple, attractive and festive. Outfit tables with linens, china, and floral arrangements. Your local stationery or party supply store, and many online boutiques, sell stylish paper goods and disposable flatware that will also work well when it comes to beautifying your tables or buffet area.

Color scheming

The simplest way to develop a cohesive theme for the baby shower is to establish a compelling color palette. These hues should be represented in the design of the invitations; then, for the actual event, select a few key elements to communicate your color story. The table linens, china or paper goods, floral arrangements and other decorations are a great place to start. Even the beverages you're offering (say, a refreshing strawberry-lemon punch or rosé Champagne) are potential participants in the scene you're creating. The same is true of your snacks and desserts—just keep in mind that a dollop of blue frosting on a cupcake is one thing, but dyed-blue tuna salad tea sandwiches will probably scare people.

Punching up pink and blue

If you know the sex of the child, your shower can certainly embrace one of the traditional gender-specific color schemes— pink for girls, blue for boys. However, you needn't feel limited to the greeting-card-industry versions of these colors, which many shower hostesses (and guests) may find uninspiring.

Here are some ways to modernize these hues.

Alternative interpretations Instead of traditional pink, try sophisticated alternatives like coral, magenta or watermelon. Consider replacing the usual sky or baby blue with navy, slate or royal blue.

One color, multiple shades Rather than sticking to one, specific hue, work within a family of colors—say, three or four different shades of pink or blue that display a range of light-to-dark values.

Mix it up Combine the standard baby-shower pink or blue with a more "grown-up" shade. Sage green and chocolate brown pair well with baby blue; dove gray and charcoal are great with cotton-candy pink.

Cute! Enclose a paint-chip strip with your invitations. Use a hole-punch and ribbon to tie a note to it asking guests to a) wrap their presents with gift-wrap in coordinating colors, and b) use the paint-chip strip as a gift tag.

Beyond the basics

Of course, you can also ignore tradition altogether and opt for a brilliant color scheme of your own choosing. Don't know the sex of the child? Adopt the same strategy. Here's where you might find inspiration for a gender-neutral color scheme.

❀ *Take a look at the baby's due date—let's say it's March—and use that month's birthstone as the foundation for your shower colors: Aquamarine—shades of aqua and/or ice blue. The mother's (or both parents') birthstone color can be used as an accent hue.*

❀ *Yellow is the default "unisex" color. Also consider hues in the turquoise, green and orange families.*

❀ *The mother's or both parents' favorite color(s) are perfectly valid sources of inspiration.*

❀ *Why not take your cue from the nursery décor that the parents have chosen?*

Cute! If you like the "birthstone" idea, give the mother-to-be a piece of jewelry that incorporates her new baby's birthstone. When the baby is born, if it's a girl, you can commemorate the occasion with a child-size ring or charm featuring the same gem—for the child to enjoy when she's older.

Cute! Instead of floral centerpieces, place small clusters of glass vases and apothecary jars on each table (or arrange a larger grouping on a centrally-located display table). Fill each vessel with a different type of candy—jelly beans, gumballs, lollipops, saltwater taffy—but make sure the candy selections conform to a specific color combination.

Attention to detail

While color is always a great jumping-off point, there are additional ways to "theme" your baby shower. Consider using the following...

Patterns Linen rental companies offer all manner of tablecloths in a variety of prints and patterns. Gingham, polka-dots, stripes, toile and pastel plaids can cover your tables or you may use them as runners atop plain white linen. Ribbons in coordinating patterns can be tied around the stems of wine glasses and used as napkin rings. If a dog or cat is present at the shower, you can tie one of these ribbons around its neck, too! People who like to decorate warn that it's easy to get carried away with patterns —too many can look busy, especially in an intimate party setting. If you must work with more than one pattern, all should conform to the same color palette. You don't want guests wondering what compelled you to pair lavender gingham napkins with a sunflower-print tablecloth.

Tasteful baby shower-appropriate themes All of the images below can appear as motifs on invitations and later, show up on table numbers, place cards, menu cards and favor tags:

- *nest and robin's egg*
- *baby animals (chicks, ducklings, bunnies, piglets, puppies, kittens)*
- *watering can and flowers*
- *cherries, strawberries, apples*
- *elephants*
- *ladybugs*
- *bees*
- *hummingbirds*
- *storks*
- *moon and stars*
- *fairies*

Some of these motifs can be represented in the favors you give. For a nest and robin's egg theme, for example, give little bird's nests filled with blue Jordan almonds or for a bunny theme, create frosted rabbit-shaped cookies.

Cute! Two seasonal motifs to consider— an acorn for autumn baby showers, and a butterfly for spring and summer showers. Acorns and butterflies can take the form of sugar decorations on a cake and faux versions can be wired onto napkin rings or affixed to a door wreath. Both are "life cycle" symbols that point to hope, growth, positive transformation and beauty, and are therefore ideal baby shower motifs.

Refreshments

If you are hiring a caterer or celebrating at a restaurant or banquet facility, you will probably be presented with a selection of menu options to choose from. When making your selections, be sure to account for any dietary restrictions you have been made aware of and if it's a multi-generational crowd, keep the fare elegant, but also familiar—this is not the time to introduce Grandma to sashimi.

While an open bar isn't necessary, it's appropriate to serve guests wine or some sort of specialty cocktail. You can save money by limiting your offerings to Prosecco and inexpensive Champagne-based cocktails like Bellinis and mimosas.

If you're preparing the refreshments yourself, simply peruse your favorite cookbooks for recipes. Consult the mother-to-be to determine her food and drink preferences—fresh-fruit smoothies, iced tea, or a colorful non-alcoholic punch may be in order. You can even organize a buffet spread and ask select guests to bring one of their signature dishes to the party. Keep in mind that if you are hosting a large crowd you may need to rent certain items like coffee/hot water urns, glassware, tiered dessert trays and a punch bowl.

Cute! How about fairy-size portions of nostalgic fare like mini grilled cheese sandwiches or shot glasses filled with ice-cold milk and topped with a crispy oatmeal cookie?

Favors

Guests always appreciate party favors, especially when they've given up a precious weekend afternoon to attend the baby shower and have come to the event bearing gifts themselves. Here are some guaranteed crowd-pleasers:

- brownies
- chocolates
- compilation CDs with song titles that include the word "baby"
- cookie cutters
- cookies
- cupcakes
- drawer sachets
- ink stamps
- jars of jam or honey
- little notebooks
- lollipops
- miniature books of poetry or inspiring quotes
- paper fans
- picture frames
- scented candles
- soaps in baby animal shapes
- tea or coffee
- tiny pitchers
- trinket or pill boxes

In lieu of, or in addition to favors, you might like to make a donation to a children's charity like UNICEF or the Make-a-Wish Foundation. Since traditional favors often skew towards the feminine, making a charity donation is a great way to honor guests at a co-ed baby shower.

Prizes

If you're playing games, have some choice prizes on hand to award winners. You may also want to have a few "door prizes" on offer—these are prizes given to guests as a result of sheer serendipity. For example, you could place a sticker underneath one or several plates at your tables. Before the showeree opens her gifts, thank everyone for coming and ask them to take a peek under their plates. Those with stickers "win." Another popular door prize: Awarding a gift to the guest whose birthday is closest to the baby's due date (you can increase the number of "winners" by awarding such a prize to one guest per table). Some prize possibilities that are universally desirable:

- *gift certificates (to a book store, coffee shop, movie theater or nail salon)*
- *toiletry gift set*
- *bottle of wine or Champagne*
- *one-size-fits-all slippers*
- *pretty stationery*
- *gourmet vinegar or olive oil*
- *fancy assorted chocolates*
- *one of the floral centerpieces decorating each table at the shower*

"Mini" showers

Lots of expecting mothers (and/or fathers) have acquaintances who do not overlap with their network of close friends. Coworkers often fall into this category, as do members of book clubs, choirs, knitting groups, and Lamaze or exercise classes. It is common for these circles to organize a "mini" baby shower attended exclusively by its members. If this is a task you would like to take on, fête the expecting parent in a low-key way. Cake and Champagne, coffee and donuts or an informal bagel brunch in an office conference room is perfectly fine. Rather than having each guest bringing his or her own gift, groups like these usually pool their resources to purchase one or two gifts. If you are organizing such a gesture, be considerate of what everyone can spend and don't be offended if some do not contribute—you may feel close to Sarah

but others in the group may barely know her and shouldn't feel obligated to participate financially. So make it clear that doing so is optional. Send an email so that no one feels put on the spot:

As you may know, Sarah Morton's last day before she goes on maternity leave is next Friday. Please set some time aside on the afternoon of Thursday, April 12th to celebrate and wish her well. Festivities will be held in the 7th floor conference room; a card will be circulating so be sure to sign it!

In addition, several of us are pitching in to get Sarah the Pack 'N Play and high chair on her baby gift registry. A contribution of $10 to $20 each would be most welcome. Please let me know if you are able to participate.

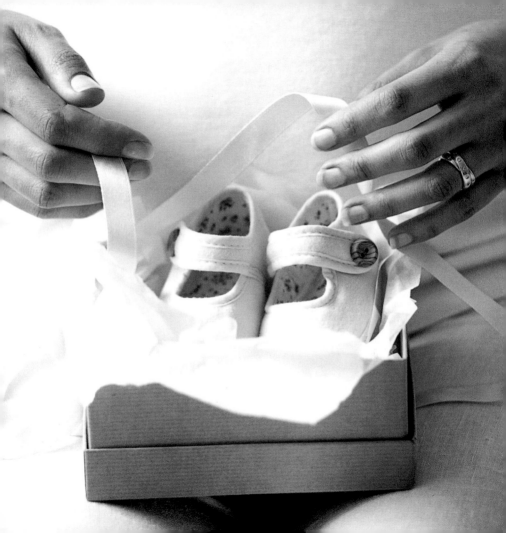

Cute! A "Baby's Library" is a great shower theme for a book club and will net the parents a bundle of books to enjoy with their child throughout the years to come. Request that each guest bring a children's book to the mini shower and write an inscription on the inside. Assign guests different age ranges so that baby's first bookshelf will be as diverse as it is delightful. Some universal favorites to consider, right:

Book it!

A Children's Garden of Verses
by Robert Louis Stevenson

Goodnight Moon
by Margaret Wise Brown

Make Way For Ducklings
by Robert McCloskey

Mr. Rabbit and the Lovely Present
by Maurice Sendak

Runaway Bunny
by Margaret Wise Brown

The Cat in the Hat by Dr. Seuss

The Madeline series
by Ludwig Bemelmans

The Tale of Peter Rabbit
by Beatrix Potter

The Velveteen Rabbit by Margery Williams and William Nicholson

Winnie the Pooh by A.A. Milne

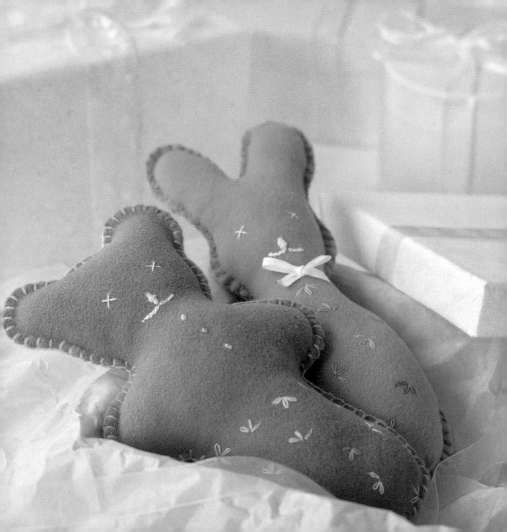

Gifts & games

Gift registries

Once your plans for the baby shower are in place, it's up to the parents-to-be to create baby gift registries at a few stores; websites are best and make it easy for out-of-towners to purchase and send gifts. New mothers-to-be should consult friends and family who have recently had babies to determine the exact products, brands and quantities to include on their registries. You may or may not be qualified to advise; at the very least, registering parents should

remember to include older babyhood items (say, a highchair, a forward-facing car seat and sippy cups), not just those for infants. One can never register for too many bibs, burp cloths or thin, soft wash cloths. Another tip: Don't register for several quantities of one type of bottle because you may have to try a few brands to see which one works best for your baby.

Gift guidance

As hostess of the shower, you may find yourself fielding an array of gift-related questions when guests call or email to RSVP. To that end, make sure you follow the guidelines, opposite:

Where the parents are registered

These days, almost everyone who accepts an invitation to a baby shower will expect to purchase their gift from an online or in-store gift registry. Whether it's a website or a physical address or both, you should know where these registries exist as well as the particulars of accessing them.

The sex of the child

Ideally, your invitations would include this information or imply that the shower is "unisex." If not, additional clarification may be needed.

How many babies are on the way

Is the person carrying twins, triplets or an even larger brood? This is something that guests will certainly find helpful when shopping for gifts because they'll know to buy in multiples.

The child's age

Applicable—and important—if you're planning a shower to celebrate an adoption.

The gifts that are already spoken for

Parents and close relatives often call dibs on significant purchases like the baby carriage, crib, bedding and changing table—guests planning to give an expensive group gift will appreciate having this information.

Any items that aren't needed

If the couple has already had a baby or two, the gear they acquired upon the birth of their first child may not need to be replaced this time around.

Shopping tips

If you find yourself in a deeper baby-gift conversation with certain guests, you may wish to volunteer the following shopping advice:

Sizes New mothers often receive a surplus of infant-size baby clothes (0 to 3 months) that they end up not being able to use because new babies tend to outgrow this size range very quickly. Encourage guests to buy clothes in larger sizes; buying in the 12 to 18 months range will set your outfit apart and practically guarantee that it gets worn (just not right away).

Season When deciding on a particular item or size, always consider the season in which baby will be wearing it. If the baby is expected in July, it doesn't make sense to buy cozy sleepers, warm coats and long-sleeved shirts in size 0 to 3 months when the weather will be hot.

Allergies If the mother is allergic to wool, she's not going to want to clothe or swaddle her baby in anything made of this material.

Practicality New parents generally agree that stuffed animals, no matter how cute and cuddly, are not as desirable as the infant care essentials they will be using on a daily basis.

Safety Stay away from glass-eyed dolls and stuffed animals and any other toys that might be harmful to baby if he/she puts them in his/her mouth.

Turn the page for more gift-giving advice, straight from savvy moms...

Cute! If the new baby has an older sibling, it's extremely thoughtful to bring this child a small gift. Nothing extravagant, but a coloring book or stuffed toy can certainly alleviate the jealousy he/she may feel upon viewing his/her new sibling's loot!

Mothers know best

"Handmade quilts are amazing!"
Rosemary

"Dresses are useless for baby girls ages 6 to 12 months. They are crawling around at this time and they can't crawl in a dress! So if guests ask, tell them to buy dresses for teeny, tiny ladybugs or in sizes 12 months and over."
Christina

"Small socks, and little shoes are useless. They look cute, but never fit and are a waste of money."
Anya

"No one *needs* a baby wipe warmer! It's the world's most *useless* invention that will clog up landfills until someone puts their *bootie* down!"
Monica

"I *loved* a gift basket a friend put together for me. It included organic baby lotion, body wash, diaper cream, and lanolin (for Mama's sore breasts!), all *wrapped up* in a *cozy* infant towel."
Jennifer

"The simplest and most useful gift I received was a pack of cloth diapers. I used them as burp cloths and ended up buying about five more packs of them. My baby throws up constantly so these rags are constantly being used."

Hillary

"Babies practically live in onesies and sleeper sacks during those first few months, so you can't go wrong tying a ribbon around a few of these!"

Lauren

"Teddy bears are useless dust mite catchers in a baby's room, and will likely have to be thrown out for hygiene reasons."

Katherine

"I received way too many swaddling blankets!"

Charlotte

"Creating a registry may seem like a lot of work, but it saves you spending hours returning unwanted gifts later."

Grace

"Gift cards are lovely—you can use them to get any items you need at the last minute."

Evy

Opening the gifts

Let's be honest, the opening of gifts is the focus of the baby shower and everyone attending is prepared to "oooh" and "ahhhh" accordingly as the showeree unwraps each and every one of those beribboned boxes. However, some showerees choose to open up gifts in private, preferring instead to spend the event socializing with guests. If your showeree is prepared to go the traditional gift-opening route, a friend or family member should be in charge of handing over each gift; once opened, it should be set aside with the card or gift-tag carefully placed inside the box. Another close friend or family member should sit alongside the mother-to-be with pen and paper (or a "gift assist," available at select stationery boutiques) to jot down each gift and the person who gave it. This important step makes the process of sending thank-you notes that much easier.

Cute! *The most wonderful and meaningful "group" gift: Many shower hostesses mail guests loose pages from a scrapbook in advance of the shower, asking them to design a page with words of advice and encouragement, along with photos and other sweet remembrances. Present the completed scrapbook at the shower, wrapped-up as a gift along with all the others. When opened, make sure the scrapbook gets passed around so that guests can see the finished product.*

Games and activities

Baby shower games encourage laughter and conversation among a crowd of guests who don't necessarily know each other well. But they're generally considered passé—most showerees and attendees find them unbearably corny, if not completely ridiculous. However, if you really want your guests to play games that involve a diaper and chocolate sauce, wrapping the mother-to-be in a roll of toilet paper or sucking down juice from a baby bottle, you'll find no shortage of options and instructions online.

In lieu of games, most guests will be amenable to taking part in an activity of some sort. At an intimate shower, one popular project you might consider is to provide each guest with a white cotton onesie to decorate with fabric paint. Offer to launder and deliver the finished "designer" garments so that the mother-to-be doesn't have to concern herself with these details. Another fun crafting project: Trace a letter of the alphabet on removable pages from a scrapbook or photo album. At the shower, give each guest a letter to decorate, supplying crayons, scissors, magic markers, stickers, glitter, and any other materials that will inspire the "artists." In the end, the mother-to-be will have baby's first "ABC" book, a keepsake as practical as it is adorable.

Cute! One game that is fun to play involves asking each guest to bring one of her own baby photos to the shower. At the event, display and number each of these photos on a bulletin board. Hand out copies of the guest list and have guests mark the number of the baby photo that corresponds to each guest's name. The player with the most correct pairings wins.

Etiquette explained

Advice and encouragement

Q *Patricia called to RSVP to our friend Betsy's baby shower—she is unable to attend and feels terrible. Is there anything she can do to feel a part of the festivities (and make it up to Betsy)?*

A Yes. Everyone who is invited to a baby shower is expected to give a gift, regardless of whether or not he or she can attend. So any guest who must decline an invite can make amends by purchasing a gift and ensuring its delivery to the mother-to-be. Patricia can certainly go this route, or even better, give her gift to Betsy in person over a fun, one-on-one "shower" that involves a delicious lunch and/or spa treatments. If Patricia wishes to participate in the festivities in absentia, her creative input may be helpful, as is a financial contribution to the party itself (maybe she'd like to pay for the flowers?).

Q *What do you do if the baby unexpectedly arrives in advance of the shower date?*

A Mother Nature's plans always trump those of the shower hostess, no matter how fabulous a celebration you've been planning. If the baby should arrive early, you will probably be among the first to know. You can proceed with the shower date and time as planned, provided Mom and baby are up to it (if her premature baby requires prolonged hospital care, she understandably may want to postpone or even cancel the affair altogether). If this is the case, your next step is to phone all guests—even those who have RSVP'd "no"—explaining the situation and that the event has been postponed until further notice. Offer to receive and deliver

baby gifts on the mother's behalf. If, heaven forbid, there is a miscarriage or another pregnancy-related tragedy, phone all guests as outlined above. Then, use all the time and energy you would have devoted to the shower toward supporting the parents and helping them heal.

Q *We wanted to throw a baby shower for friends of ours who are in the process of adopting a child. Will anyone think this is weird?*

A Adopting parents need and deserve all the support—and baby gear—that biological parents do, so your idea to fête them with a shower is not only lovely, but perfectly appropriate. Encourage the parents to register for gifts, but wait to schedule the shower until the child is officially in their care. The invitations you send should include the name, age and sex of the child.

Q *A co-worker remarked that she thinks moms who have showers for second, third and fourth babies are tacky. Will guests be offended if I organize a shower for the birth of my sister Sarah's second child*

A Some guests might think, "I gave Sarah a car seat for her first baby, why does she need a new one?" Most guests, however, delight in celebrating the birth of a child and will be glad for an excuse to shop for and proffer additional baby gifts. The gifts at "repeat" showers tend to be less expensive and more indulgent than practical (a toy or an outfit instead of a playpen or highchair) and the shower itself is usually more intimate and low-key in nature. But it's definitely an event worth celebrating in whatever manner you choose, so don't let other people's opinions discourage you.

UK Stockists

INVITATIONS & BIRTH ANNOUNCEMENTS

www.cardsselect.co.uk
www.mooksdesign.co.uk

BABY GIFT REGISTRIES

www.mamasandpapas.co.uk
www.johnlewis.com

FAVORS & DECORATIONS

www.showermybaby.co.uk
www.babyshowerhost.co.uk
www.babyshowercentre.co.uk

BABY CLOTHES, FURNITURE & OTHER GIFTS

www.Sprogbox.co.uk
www.babyboxlondon.com
www.theflowerstork.com
www.babycity.co.uk
www.bloomingmarvellous.co.uk
www.urchin.co.uk
www.georgieandtom.co.uk
www.uniquebabygifts.co.uk
www.kuati.com
www.allthingsgreen.net
www.jojomamanbebe.co.uk
www.tuttibambini.co.uk
www.toysRus.co.uk
www.mothercare.com

GIFT WRAP & RIBBON

www.paperchase.co.uk
www.clintoncards.co.uk

US Stockists

INVITATIONS & BIRTH ANNOUNCEMENTS

www.finestationery.com
www.bumbleink.com
Kate Spade Baby (at
www.crane.com)

BABY GIFT REGISTRIES

www.buybuybaby.com
www.babiesRus.com
www.babygap.com
www.potterybarnkids.com
www.babystyle.com

FAVORS

www.ababyshower.com/favors
www.beau-coup.com
www.favorsbylisa.com
www.laburdick.com
Luxury chocolates in mice, rabbit, bee and penguin shapes

Eleni's
(www.elenis.com)
Adorable frosted sugar cookies

Pete's Gourmet Confections
(www.petesgourmet.com)
Homemade marshmallows

FAVOR PACKAGING & EMBELLISHMENTS

Lucky Onion
(www.luckyonion.com)
Will customize box and paper colors, and patterns

Paper Source
(www.paper-source.com)
Ink stamps galore and countless little boxes

www.myownlabels.com
Pretty personalized labels for jars of jam or honey

NURSERY FURNITURE

www.modernnursery.com
www.adrianaprimadonna.com
www.bellini.com

DECORATIONS

www.plumparty.com
www.orientaltrading.com

Michaels
(www.michaels.com)

GIFT WRAP & RIBBON

Tinsel Trading Company
(www.tinseltrading.com)

Hello Lucky
(www.hellolucky.com)

Whimsy Press
(www.whimsypress.com)

Romantic Flowers
(www.romanticflowers.com)

UNIQUE BABY GIFTS

www.vivre.com
www.miabossi.com
www.babyaulait.com
www.etsy.com

Index

Picture credits